NO PULLING ALLOWED:

From Painfully Disappointing Drag to Delightfully Relaxing Stroll

Natasja Lewis DipCABT

Published by
Elite Publishing Academy
www.ElitePublishingAcademy.com

First Edition published 2019

Printed and bound in Great Britain
www.ElitePublishingAcademy.com

A catalogue record for this book is available from The British Library

ISBN 978-1-912713-86-8

Dedication

For my dad for his eternal support and love. I will miss you to the end of my days.

Table of Contents

Praise

What dog professionals are saying about this book.

5 stars. This is a fantastic read for anyone struggling to get their dog to walk nicely on the lead. Not only does Natasja explain in great detail how it isn't just about getting a loose lead, you also get a five-step process for success with really useful games attached. Lots of amazing life experience stories in there, that you just don't find in many other books.

Claire Lawrence, Dog Trainer www.highpeakdogs.co.uk

As a dog walker I come across many dogs who pull on the lead. Their owners tell me that they've tried everything, head collars, harnesses and the such. But they haven't tried to train the dog to loose lead. Natasja will give you all the ingredients to train your dog to walk calmly by your side. She shows you how to do this in a way that you can easily implement yourself. Yes, it takes some commitment but if you've brought this book then you are willing. I shall certainly be buying this book for some of my customers!

Sally Cousins, Dog Walker www.wooferswalkies.co.uk

Pulling is a major problem in the canine world. For an owner with this problem, it's very frustrating and nothing seems to make a difference. There's no book that addresses this problem or helps you understand why your dog pulls. Until now, 'no pulling allowed' is an enjoyable book that really helps you implement steps to improve your dog's pulling and makes you see that there is light at the end of the tunnel. Thanks, Natasja!

Harriett Goodall, Dog Walker www.pawtasticpetsitting.co.uk

Fun, Focus, Play; a development programme with a difference! You won't find any boring instruction-manual-style training here, no repetitive sits or downs.

Instead this is concept training. It's about shaping dogs' emotional responses so that they are more comfortable and better able to cope with all aspects of life. It's about giving dogs the life skills they need to solve everyday problems by making the handler more exciting than the distractions in the environment.

Natasja weaves her advice amongst entertaining stories and unexpected memorable analogies. What has The Good, The Bad and the Ugly got to do with dog training? You'll have to read to find out.

Follow Natasja's method and you will see an improvement in your dog's behaviour while building a bond through reward and game-based training.

Katie Guastapaglia, Enrichment Specialist at Dogwood Adventure Play www.dogwoodadventureplay.com

Acknowledgements

I would like to use this page to thank those people who supported me during the long months it took me to write this book.

First and foremost, my heartfelt thanks go to my wonderful and long-suffering husband Paul, who put up with my antics while writing this book, who helped me with my final edit and checked my manuscript to make sure everything made sense.

Dank-je-wel, to Dom and Vicky, my mentors, who held my hand throughout this project, offering suggestions and advice. I don't think I could have finished this project without your encouragement.

Carol Bentley, a friend in a million, and proof-reader extraordinaire, thank you for doing such a great job!

To the Diamond Girls who Beta Read my book and offered such helpful feedback; I want to say *Grazie Mille.*

Danke to Julia Brown of Brown Owl Designs for the lovely cover designs.

To Alex Wardle and Chris Brignell for the photos featured in this book - *Merci.*

Thanks to Bill Goss of Elite Publishing Academy for doing such a lovely job of printing my book.

To Wendy Halliday for fighting with my manuscript and for being the best assistant any dog trainer could ask for.

Dog walking and dog training icons made by Freepik from www.flaticon.com.

And to you, dear Reader, I say - Thank you for picking up this book and making the effort to improve your relationship with your dog. If you enjoyed reading this book and found my advice helpful, please leave a review on Amazon or Audible for me. A nice review will allow me to help other dog owners that are struggling with their dog's lead walking, just as you were when you first started your journey with me.

Thank you all for believing in me.

Natasja x

Conceiving "No Pulling Allowed"

When I first started to write this book, I didn't really have a clear vision of where it would lead me. I wanted to write a book about how to teach a dog to walk on a loose lead, but then I started to think about the daily dog walk and the struggles a lot of dog owners, like yourself, face when taking your dogs out.

I considered covering all aspects of a dog walk, not just how to teach a dog to walk on the lead.

I thought about including off lead control, calling your dog to come back to you and even touch on how to teach your dog to greet other dogs and people when she is off the lead.

For a long time, I struggled with how to make this book work.

Then I had an epiphany:

I could write about all these topics in one big book. Touching on each item in turn and do an adequate job of teaching you. Or I could concentrate on one single problem and cover the related subjects in much more detail.

I chose the latter option.

By concentrating on showing you how you can stop your dog from pulling on the lead and by teaching you how to create a dog that wants to walk with you, I was able to cover the subject matter in much greater detail.

It is still my intention to cover the other subjects such as how to teach your dog to come back when called, and how to have off lead control and appropriate greeting behaviour in the future. To do this I have decided to write a series of **Fun | Focus | Play** dog training books. No Pulling Allowed is the first book in this new series of dog training books.

This is in no way a traditional reward-based training book. My methods go beyond the limitations that are experienced by people whose dogs are just not interested in food rewards. Don't get me wrong, food rewards still play a big part in my **Fun | Focus | Play** method, but we use them in a different way as well as utilising environmental and play rewards.

Intrigued?

You should be!

Let me show you how my training method works and how it can change you and your dog's life.

One last thing before I let you get your teeth into this little book of mine. I like to refer to dogs by their name however for ease of reading, I decided to use "she" when referring to dogs in this book.

I hope you enjoy reading this book and wish you many hours of walking fun with your best friend by your side.

Leave the frustration behind and embrace the future.

Natasja x

How To Achieve The Perfect Walk

We all strive to have those lovely relaxing saunters where you enjoy your dog's company strolling along the pathways in your local field or forest. But this is not how walks are for many dog owners.

All around the world, shoulders are being pulled out of their sockets, elbows are jarred, and did you know that you can actually end up with tennis elbow from a pulling dog?

No? Let me explain.

A Pleasant Walk, Gone Bad

Some years ago, I was looking after a whippet and a greyhound for a client. They were lovely dogs, but unfortunately, they were lead pullers.

On this occasion, the greyhound had cut her leg a few days earlier and, sporting a lovely even row of stitches, was confined to lead walking exercise only.

I took them both on a nice walk through our local fields along the River Stour. All was well, and I had let the whippet off the lead as he was a sensible lad who loved racing around the field chasing imaginary bunnies, while I had kept his companion on her leash.

But things soon changed as another dog walker came into view. Her dog was off the lead, and she was throwing a ball. Not a problem usually, but as I had the greyhound on a lead, I shouted to the dog walker asking her to stop throwing the ball as she went by.

My charge had spotted the ball, and playing fetch was one of her favourite games. This meant that she was starting to get a little fired up. I heaved a sigh of relief as the dog walker picked up the ball and stopped throwing it for her dog as she came closer, I was able to have a little chat with her explaining the situation.

All was well until we parted ways. I had not gone 10 yards before the ball whizzed over my head. My charge spotted the ball flying through the air and I quickly discovered that she, being a greyhound, was able to go from a gentle stroll to 200 mph in just 3 paces.

I can tell you as she hit the end of her lead it felt like my arm was being ripped from my body. The jolt was so powerful that before I realised what was happening, I found myself face first on the ground being dragged by a now over excited greyhound.

I ended up going to A & E that evening as the pain in my arm was excruciating. After a series of x-rays and other tests, it was determined that nothing was broken, but there was ligament damage. An appointment with the physiotherapy department was arranged and it turned out that the injury I had sustained was tennis elbow.

Injuries like this are more common than you might realise, and what starts out as a pleasant walk can quickly turn into a nightmare.

Of course, it doesn't have to be that way.

My Perfect Walk

One February morning a few years back, Paul, my husband, and I decided to take our dogs for a walk. The sun was shining and there wasn't a cloud in the sky. Perfect weather for a walk on the beach. It was a bit chilly, but we weren't complaining. For the time of year it was an absolutely gorgeous day.

We loaded ourselves and the dogs into the car and drove down to Studland Beach. We are fortunate to live in the Dorset countryside with some lovely dog-friendly beaches right on our doorstep.

If you have never been to Studland Beach let me set the scene for you. The lovely golden sand stretches for miles and miles. The waves gently lap up on the shore and at low tide the beach becomes a playground for locals and dog walkers alike.

The sand dunes are covered in the typical harsh grass type vegetation and are crisscrossed with tracks and wider paths to explore at will.

It really is the perfect spot for the ideal dog walk, and dog owners get to enjoy the beach, sea and dunes together with their canine best friends.

We arrived at the beach and unloaded the dogs, grabbed a few tennis balls and plenty of poo bags and off we went.

It was a busy day, the weather was truly exceptional, and it was heating up rapidly in the sun. There had been a slight breeze when we set off, but as the sun continued to beat down on us, our coats were off, and we were down to our t-shirts.

The dogs were enjoying running around dashing in and out the water, playing with their tennis balls as we went.

Even though there were lots of other dog walkers and dogs around, my dogs chose to stay and play with us.

Other dogs ran up to ours to say hello and the greetings were sometimes enthusiastic, resulting in a little play session, and calm and measured at other times. There was no friction, no raised heckles or even a growl.

When it was time to walk on, we just said, "let's go" and our dogs came with us straight away.

We walked from the North Beach all the way to the Studland Ferry, with the waves gently lapping up on the beach next to us.

On the way back we walked through the dunes. It was merely the perfect dog walk which left both humans and dogs feeling relaxed, refreshed and contented.

For me, the perfect dog walk is one where my dogs walk nicely next to me, especially where they need to be on the lead, and without them reacting to other dogs, people or things that are going on around them.

When they are off the lead, I want them to stay close to me, listening to my requests and engaging with me rather than going off to follow scents or to hunt for the nearest rabbit or pheasant.

If there are other people and dogs around, I want my dogs to stay with me and not run off, or at least come back to me the moment they are requested to do so, and then stay with me, without me having to nag them continually.

The Perfect Dog Walk Formula

To achieve the perfect dog walk there are 4 separate skills that my dogs and I need to master, and these are:

1. Loose Lead Walking
2. Reliable Recall
3. Off Lead Control
4. Greeting Behaviour

During this **Fun | Focus | Play** dog training series we will look at these skills separately. In this first book, we are going to have a closer look at how to get your dog to walk with you, rather than pulling you from pillar to post.

Let's go together and embark on a little journey of discovery, looking at each of the skills that you need to teach your dog to stop her from pulling on the lead.

We are going to do this by delving into what makes your dog tick and how we can use this knowledge to our advantage.

What Is The **Fun | Focus | Play** Canine Development Program?

I got my first dog, a male Shetland Sheepdog called Dali, over 25 years ago. In fact, he was my first wedding anniversary present from my hubby.

Now I know that traditionally a first wedding anniversary present is supposed to be paper, so I wondered if my husband realised this. That was until Paul presented me with Dali's documents in a pretty envelope, naming me as his owner.

The Early Days

In those days, dog training as we know it today was in its infancy. The old dominance based, Barbara Woodhouse-style of training, had been dominating the dog training scene for 20 or so years.

The mindset of the old-style dog trainers was that dogs needed to be dominated and shown who was the boss by using punishment rather than rewards to train them.

This training method slowly started to fall into disrepute, and the days when we used ear pinches and tugs on the lead to keep the dogs in line were disappearing. Instead we were moving towards using food to reward the dogs for getting it right.

I said a very relieved goodbye to those draconian training methods and embraced reward-based methods instead. The old ways never sat well with me, though the older instructors at the dog club I attended with my first dog still trained this way.

Introducing Reward Based Training

I was lucky that the more moderate trainers at the club advocated the use of rewards rather than punishment to train my dog, and I followed their example.

I whole-heartedly embraced the new reward-based methods that were being promoted by the more progressive dog trainers of the time. However, I still felt that improvements could be made.

For years I have felt that there was a vital ingredient missing with reward-based training methods. I loved the way the dogs were being rewarded for doing what we ask of them, instead of being punished for not understanding. But something was missing.

I wanted my Sheltie, Dali, to have as much fun as I was having training him, and I just wasn't feeling it. Yes, he was doing what I wanted. The method I was using was kind and fair, but still, it didn't feel quite right to me.

Looking at the competitive dog world I discovered motivational and reward-based dog training. This meant that I was now using toys as well as treats to reward Dali for doing as I asked. This was a little better, but I still felt that my dog was getting frustrated when he could not figure out what I was trying to teach him.

The Clicker Revolution

Then clicker training came along. Clicker training was the brainchild of Keller Breland, Marian Breland Bailey and Bob Bailey who developed this unique way of communicating with dolphins and other marine mammals. It allowed them to interact with their charges and administer health care.

Clicker training was introduced to the dog training world by Karen Pryor who learnt the principles of this exciting new development in animal training from them.

For those of you who haven't heard of clicker training before, let me explain what it is all about.

When we are training dogs, we sometimes struggle to get the dog to understand what we are rewarding. The clicker is a small plastic box with a metal strip in it which when pressed makes a double click noise. You use this sound to let your dog know when she has done something right. By clicking at the precise moment she does something we like and then rewarding her, we are telling her exactly what she did right. It makes figuring out what we want much easier for the dog.

The click marks the behaviour the dog is being rewarded for.

This came closer to what I was looking for. And Dali seemed to be enjoying the learning process better when I used the clicker to mark the behaviour I wanted to reward.

This resulted in him understanding what I was asking quicker and his learning became faster and faster.

But it still didn't feel quite right.

My dog was now enjoying the training better, but I wanted him not just to want to work with me because I asked, but I wanted him to enjoy learning to perform the tasks because he was having FUN. I was still not convinced that my dog was having as much fun learning and training together as I was.

I wanted him to really want to do the training we did together, I wanted the exercises to be rewarding for him because he had FUN doing it. And I wanted him to choose to work with me, not because he was being rewarded for performing the behaviours, but because he enjoyed it as much as I did.

The New Concept On The Block

Fast forward a few years and as well as having added a few more dogs to my family, I came across a few dog trainers that were doing things a little differently. They used a training method that combined clicker training with motivational reward-based training methods and gave the dogs a choice on whether they wanted to interact.

I had stumbled across a new training method called Concept Training and with it a FUN new way to teach my dogs using PLAY to create a level of FOCUS in my dogs that I had never come across before.

I started experimenting with this new method. My own dogs were my guinea pigs, and I was loving the results I was getting.

The big bonus was that it was apparent that my dogs enjoyed training time. For the first time since I started on my journey I could see that they were having fun. So much so that they will now actively ask me for training sessions. They just cannot get enough of it!

Seeing this exciting level of success in my own dogs and their eagerness to engage in our training sessions, I started to incorporate this method into my classes. Seeing similar results with my students and their dogs, I developed my own canine development program which combines the best bits of all the training methods that I have learnt from in the past.

Developing My Own Approach

I came up with my own unique blend of reward and game-based training that makes learning **FUN** for both dog and owner and, by creating **FOCUS** through **PLAY**, I have started to make a big difference in the lives of my clients and their dogs.

The **Fun | Focus | Play** canine development program was born.

You might not have heard of Concept Training before. In fact, I imagine you may not have even considered teaching your dog through games. So let me explain what Concept Training is and you will start to understand why it is such a powerful dog training tool. And why I have put its fundamentals at the heart of my own **Fun | Focus | Play** canine development program.

Concept Training is different from traditional training methods because it does not teach specific behaviours to the dog, but instead it teaches the dog life skills. This means that instead of training specific behaviours like a sit or a down, what we do instead is teach her a series of concepts.

The concepts we teach are:

- Focus
- Closeness
- Learning to deal with Frustration
- Resilience
- Optimism
- Adaptability
- Independence
- Perseverance
- Self-Control
- Reward Switching
- Calmness
- Excitement Control
- Generalisation

All these life skills are taught using the all-important games.

Through teaching these concepts, we shape the dog's emotional responses and ultimately their personalities to produce the dog that we want.

It doesn't matter if the dog is destined to be your companion, best friend, or your next obedience or agility champion, this way of training is aimed to produce a dog that is comfortable with, and can cope, in all situations and, as a result, is a joy to live with.

The Theory In A Nutshell

You might not be hugely interested in the theory behind my **Fun | Focus | Play** program, but I believe that in order to understand why teaching life skills instead of set behaviours is so powerful, we do need to touch on it. However, I will try and keep it as simple, straightforward and as short as possible. After all, I don't want to bore you to death!

Playing With Fire

I still remember the day my ma started to teach me to cook. It was a sunny spring day, and I must have been about 9 or 10. Ma was returning to work, and because she wouldn't be there when I came home from school, she wanted to teach me to cook some of the basics.

She wanted to give me enough basic knowledge of cooking that I could make my brother and me a meal if need be.

I remember being so incredibly excited because I was going to be allowed to get the gas cooker going.

I got to play with fire!

I must admit that excitement wasn't the only thing I felt that day, I felt apprehensive and even a tiny bit scared.

Putting a flame to the gas was nerve-racking. I needed to turn on the gas, light a match and then touch that match to the stove.

Whoosh!

For a moment there was a massive flame and my ma quickly turned the gas knob down a bit. I could feel my heart beating… Boom, Boom, Boom.

That was pretty scary.

Before we did anything else, my mum showed me how to control the flame using the knobs on the front of the cooker. To make sure that the pan would slowly come to a boil, rather than turning it into a heap of buckled metal in a raging fire. A pot could be ruined in just a few short minutes.

This was one of the skills I had to master before any cooking could commence.

I know it seems silly now, boiling a pan of water and dropping an egg into the rolling bubbles and making toast is not a big deal. But for a child it was really amazing, I felt like my mum was trusting me to do magic.

Over the following weeks, she taught me to cook other things too. She taught me enough to have a solid understanding of what preparing a meal was all about. Once I mastered that, we started on baking cakes.

I could continue by telling you about the first time I actually made a meal for me and my brother. It was a disaster, with smoking, melted plastic mixed in with our boil-in-the-bag Chicken Satay. I still blame my brother for that fiasco, he was the one that put the bags in the pan and put the lid on telling me all I had to do was heat it up. He never mentioned that he hadn't put water in the pan!

What I need you to understand is that what my mum did that day when she first started teaching me how to cook was give me a skill that I could use for the rest of my life. She taught me an important life skill, one that would ensure my survival.

Cooking is a life skill.

This basic skill can be applied no matter what I am cooking or what kind of cooker I am using. It doesn't matter how the cooker is powered; whether it is electrical or even a wood-fired AGA: the skills I need to cook a meal are instilled in me, and because my ma taught me this skill of cooking, I am able to provide for my family, no matter where I am.

Why Teaching Life Skills Works

This principle of teaching life skills is one of the fundamentals that my dog training program is based on.

By teaching a dog life skills rather than a set of specific behaviours, she will be able to adapt what I have taught her and apply it to many different situations and environments. And the really cool thing about it is that teaching life skills helps us shape our dog's personality too.

Yes, you heard me right.

Through teaching life skills, we are able to influence the choices that our dog makes every single day. And, as a result, we can change our dog's personality. This method works for every dog.

Just in case you are wondering whether I have gone stark raving mad, teaching life skills rather than set behaviours is fully supported by the latest discoveries in behavioural science. This method has a solid base in Learning Theory, and it takes into account our dog's emotional wellbeing too.

I want to explain this a little more, so please bear with me. I promise I won't make it too technical and boring.

Who I am today has been influenced by the experiences I had as a child. The values my parents and teachers taught me, the relationships I had with my peers and the culture I grew up in. The experiences I have had in my life and choices I have made, as a result of what I have been taught over the years, is what makes me, ME.

Everything I do, who I admire and how I respond to different situations is influenced by my personality.

And it is no different for our dogs.

Their personalities are influenced and changed by the life lessons and life skills they learn along the way. Their previous experiences have a significant bearing on how they react and the choices they make when faced with challenging situations.

The really cool thing for you as your dog's owner, parent figure, teacher, playmate and friend, is that by influencing and steering your dog's choices to the ones that you want her to make, you can change her personality. This means that the decisions you want your dog to make become the default choices your dog will start to choose.

The only thing you need to do is to teach her the life skills she needs to make those correct choices.

Summary

Your dog's personality is determined by the choices she makes every single day. By teaching your dog life skills, you are influencing the decisions she makes. Because you are affecting the choices she makes through games and exercises, you are shaping your dog's personality.

Your dog's personality is fluid and not set in stone, you can influence how your dog thinks and reacts.

Remember:

You can teach your dog set behaviours or life skills.

Life skills are more adaptable than taught behaviours such as a sit, down or stay, and have more influence on your dog's overall behaviour and personality.

Action Point:

Try to spot when your dog makes a good choice when at home. For example: you are making dinner and instead of being under your feet she has settled on her bed. Make sure you reward her for this fabulous choice.

Why Do We Work?

Have you ever seriously thought about the one question that is probably on everyone's mind as they hit the snooze button on their alarm clock every morning?

"Why should I get up and go to work?"

Why do we crawl out of bed each and every morning?

Why not roll over and stay in bed until we feel ready to face the day?

Why not fill our days with fun adventure and do the stuff we desperately want to do instead?

Why not enjoy living life to the fullest without a care in the world, every single day of our lives?

Perhaps you love the feeling of being in control because you enjoy the responsibility your work brings you. Maybe you really enjoy the challenge that your job gives you. Or you love and appreciate the daily social interactions with your colleagues, and that is the reason you go to work every day.

Why Work?

I read a fascinating article by leading psychology professor Barry Schwartz as I was researching this chapter. It was called "why work?" and was based on his TED talk "The way we think about work is broken" which was featured on the non-profit's TED (Technology Entertainment and Design Conference) website last year.

It actually made me wonder about what motivates us to get up every morning.

There is no way for me to know what exactly it is that motivates you to get up. Each person's motivation is personal to them. Though I can probably have a good guess at what yours is likely to be.

The one single thing that, for most of us, will play a big part in our motivation is that we need to make money. Money helps us to afford the finer things that make our lives worth living.

The wages we get as a reward for doing our job is an excellent motivator for most of us.

It should not surprise you that dogs are a lot like humans. Dogs need proper motivation too. They need us to reward them for doing the things we ask of them.

It is our job as their teacher, parent figure or owner to find the things they find motivating and rewarding. This will then help us to influence and shape their behaviour.

How To Motivate Your Dog

The easiest way to motivate your dog and to help us shape her behaviour is by making sure that we reward her for doing the things we want to see more of.

By rewarding your dog more, she will become more motivated to choose those behaviours that we want her to learn.

Now you might be wondering "how do I find out what motivates my dog and what reward will she be willing to work for?"

Well, the obvious answer is to ask your dog!

And that is precisely what you should be doing.

You don't have to be Sherlock Holmes to figure out what motivates her, and which rewards work best, but there are a few simple tests that you can do to find out what makes your dog tick.

You will already know if your dog likes food, and I am here to tell you that all healthy dogs love to eat. If your dog doesn't appear to be interested in food, then either you are not using the right foodstuffs, or your dog simply isn't hungry.

The only thing we need to figure out is what her favourite and least favourite foods are so that we can start using them to our advantage!

This is extremely easy to do. All you need to do is cobble together a suitable selection of different foods from your store cupboard and fridge. Then ask your dog which food items she prefers.

For example, you could put together a selection of food items like this:

- A portion of your dog's normal food.
- A selection of store-bought treats.
- Pieces of cooked or dried liver.
- Meaty pieces of left-over roast.
- Cubes of cheese
- Etc.

Now we ask your dog which her favourite is. The simplest way to do this is to offer your dog two different treats, hide one in each hand and let your dog sniff both hands and then make her choose which treat she wants. Reward her by opening the hand she indicated, letting her eat the contents. Write down the results.

Now repeat by offering the next two treats until you have graded all the different rewards from 1 to 10 with 1 being the least favoured treat and 10 the treat your dog desires the most.

And we can do the same with toys.

Grab a wide variety of dog toys and play with your dog, play with her indoors and in your garden. Which of these toys does she really love to play with? I am sure that your dog will let you know pretty quickly what her favourite toy is.

Once you have figured out which your dog's favourite toys are at home, you can then take these toys to a local field, park or beach and try playing with her there.

Is your dog as interested in these toys in this new place as she is at home? Is there one toy she cannot resist playing with? If so, then great, as you can use that toy to reward your dog when you are out and about.

It is good to note that there are other things you can use to reward your dog. You can also use verbal praise, scratches behind her ears or a cuddle. Even offering her a drink can be rewarding, if that is what she desires most at that particular point in time.

One thing I must tell you about rewards is how much your dog desires the reward we are offering depends on the level of distractions present at that particular time.

If there are a lot of distractions, your dog will need a more exciting and higher value reward.

You will find that you can get away with using a lower value reward when you are at home and in a familiar environment. But when you are at the park, field or beach where there will be lots of distractions - like other people and dogs, livestock or rabbits, deer and birds - you will need to use higher value rewards.

Summary

Your dog needs to be motivated to work with us. However, what drives your dog will be personal to her.

It is your job as your dog's owner and teacher to figure out what motivates her.

Once you figure out what motivates your dog, you can use it to reward her.

The rewards on offer need to be something that your dog desires.

Considering which rewards will work best for your dog is a crucial part of working out your training plan. In fact, I would say it is vital to your success in training your dog.

You will need to use higher value rewards in more challenging situations.

Action Point:

Sit down with your dog and work out what her favourite food rewards are, and which toys she loves to play with both at home, in the garden and when out on a walk. Make sure you make a note of your findings as this information is invaluable!

Why Does My Dog Pull On The Lead?

Your dog might be perfectly happy to walk by your side when she is not on a lead. However, the moment you clip that lead onto her collar she drags you from pillar to post. This is very frustrating for you, as well as being darned uncomfortable on your arm and shoulder and perhaps even painful on your back.

So why do dogs pull on a lead?

The simplest explanation of why dogs pull on the lead is because we actually teach them to do it without realising.

"Now, how can that be?", I hear you ask.

Well, let me explain.

Introducing The Lead: What Can Go Wrong?

The very first time you put a lead on your new puppy you allow her to walk wherever she wants. You let her decide where she wants to go and follow meekly behind her holding on to the lead.

Your puppy has spotted a leaf fluttering by and decides that chasing the leaf is a great game. You try and keep up but inevitably as your puppy pounces and darts after the leaf, the lead goes tight. Pup is now experiencing pressure on her delicate little neck for the first time, and she does not like the sensation.

Instinctively she starts to fight against this pressure. Feeling trapped, she pulls to get away from the pressure. You hate to see her in distress, so you keep hold of the lead and follow. Trying to release the tension in the lead because you don't want her to hurt herself.

Now fast forwards a few days. You are lead training your puppy again. Now as soon as the lead goes on, puppy tries to pull away. You put a little tension in the lead as you are trying to teach her to follow you, instead of you following her.

Your puppy remembers the pressure she felt on her little neck the first time she had the lead on. She didn't like it, so she starts to fight against the force. You apply a little more tension to the lead to get her to come to you, and your puppy responds by fighting even harder.

One of two things is likely to happen here.

Scenario 1:

She pulls and strains and shakes her little head and somehow, fighting against the pressure, she manages to pull out of her small puppy collar.

Wow, what a relief! All that nasty pressure is gone. Your puppy has now learnt that if she fights hard enough, she will gain freedom.

Scenario 2:

Puppy pulls and strains and because you don't want her to hurt herself you rush forward to release the pressure. Here your puppy learns that if she pulls you keep following her, so she gets to go wherever she wants to go, and she will get there quicker.

What happened?

Every Action Has An Equal And Opposite Reaction

In both scenarios, we are dealing with this little instinct called Opposition Reflex. This is an automatic response, a reflex that causes us and our dogs to resist pressure with an equal (or greater) force.

Just think about what happens if someone leans into you, you don't fall over, do you?

This is because of the opposition reflex, without having to think about it you instinctively match the force that is being put on you by the leaning.

Sometimes the solution to this problem can be as simple as preventing the opposition reflex from happening. This can be by changing from a collar and lead combination to a head collar or even a harness and lead combo. While changing the equipment you use can have a positive effect, it will not solve the problem in the long term.

This is because there are other reasons why dogs pull and if these are not addressed your dog will learn to pull on a harness and head collar too.

Running Away With The Horses

Remember when you were a kid, and you got fascinated by things? You got so attracted by something you saw or something you wanted, that you forgot all about what you were supposed to be doing? Well, this happened to me as a young girl.

My mum still tells this story now about how I became so obsessed with horses that I would disappear for hours on end without my mum knowing where I was.

Most of the time this wasn't a problem as I always turned up when it was time for dinner. But on this one occasion, I was so engrossed in watching the horses that I lost all track of time, and the fact that I was supposed to be running an errand for my mum.

You see my mum had asked me to pop over to Granddad's to go and get a dozen eggs from the chickens that we kept on the farm.

So, I went on my way, making a detour to the local playing fields checking to see if any of my friends were around. They weren't so I decided to go and see if the horses I so admired were in their field.

Of course, being a kid, I didn't really have any concept of how much time was passing as I was too engrossed in watching the horses.

A few days earlier I had met a young horse rider and her pony at the local playing fields, and all I wanted to do was to see if she was around. She kept her pony at the end of my Granddad's road, so I decided to go there first to see if she was around.

I was fascinated by her pony and wanted to learn more about these exquisite animals. I had asked if I could come to see her and her pony and help out. I didn't care what I had to do as long as I could spend some time around horses.

As it happened, she wasn't around, and the pony was not in the field.

In the meantime, my mum was getting worried as I had now been gone for a lot longer than she was expecting, and there still was no sign of me returning. She sent my older brother to go and look for me.

My brother went to Granddad first. Of course, he hadn't seen me. I hadn't been there yet. My brother ended up looking all over the village for me, checking in with all my friends, the local playing fields and park.

Meanwhile, disappointedly I headed towards my Granddad's. On my way, I passed a field that had previously been empty, but today two new horses had appeared.

These two pure white horses had luscious long flowing manes. The most beautiful horses I had ever laid my eyes on.

They were magnificent and the pony and his young owner I'd been looking for were quickly forgotten in that split second that I looked into their gorgeous eyes. I was enthralled, I don't know how long I stood there just watching these two horses prance about their lush green pasture.

Eventually, my brother found me there. I hadn't just become fascinated by horses, no I had become obsessed.

Unhealthy Obsessions

Getting obsessed is something that can happen to your dog too.

Dogs can become obsessed with going to the park or beach because that is where exciting things happen. The prospect of being able to play with other dogs becomes such a strong pull that your dog will drag you to the park or beach.

And then we have distractions. Different environments present different distractions for your dog:

- At the beach, there are lots of other dogs and people as well as sea birds to play with and chase. There is water to paddle in and loose sand shifting under their paws making it irresistible for your dog not to start running and bouncing around.

- In the woods, there are squirrels, deer, rabbits, pheasants to chase, and lots of interesting smells to explore and trails to follow.

Your dog will be desperate to go and explore all these exciting things. In her eagerness to get where she wants to go she pulls. Because, the way your dog sees it, pulling will get her access to the things she wants quicker.

When you are teaching your dog to walk on a nice loose lead, you need to take all these struggles into account.

You need to teach your dog some life skills that will teach her to adapt to the ever-changing environment and situations that she will come across in her life with us.

Just think about it. If we didn't have our life skills, the ones that we were taught from a young age, skills such as patience, self-control and perseverance, then we would not be able to survive and be successful in this modern world. We would be truly lost and unable to live our lives the way we do today.

Summary

There are three main reasons why dogs pull:

- Opposition Reflex, this is a purely automatic response that causes us to resist pressure.
- Because you have inadvertently taught your dog to pull on the lead.
- Dogs can become obsessed with other dogs, people or even the park or field and will pull to get access to these things quicker.

We need to teach your dog some crucial life skills to help you educate her not to pull. The life skills you need to develop in your dog are patience, self-control and perseverance.

Action Point:

Whatever the reason is that your dog is pulling on the lead, there is a very small and effective change you can make right now, even before we start teaching your dog to walk on a loose lead.

Try to catch your dog looking at you when you are going for a walk and reward her with a tasty treat or game with her favourite toy.

Eyes For Me, Only

Keeping focus in our lives is something that we all struggle with from time to time, take the renovations my husband and I are doing to our cottage, for example.

Why We Need Focus

Five years ago, we were very excited to buy a lovely little cottage that had been built in the 1800s. But sadly, we underestimated the scale of the renovations and improvements that our new home needed.

Full of enthusiasm and thinking we had a good idea of what was needed, we rushed headfirst into the restoration project. We were brimming with ideas for improvements and visions of our little warren of a cottage restored to its former glory.

We looked past the rotten windows, lack of central heating and the leaking kitchen roof.

The cottage had an old Rayburn that provided hot water and a way to cook our meals. There were a few storage heaters downstairs and two wood burners, but shockingly no heating upstairs. Of the two bathrooms, one had a shower which fell apart the first time I tried to use it. The other one was so neglected that only a trickle of water escaped from the shower head. It was barely enough to have a proper wash.

We certainly wondered whether we had made the biggest mistake in our lives!

We decided to make a start on the renovations and first on our list of must-do-now jobs was to sort out the rotten windows. The day after we moved in, we arranged for the windows to be replaced by modern lookalike windows. The next two jobs on our "must-do-now" list were not so easy to sort out.

The heating was a challenge. Our cottage is in a very small rural village which does not have access to mains gas, so we needed to research our options.

As for the leaking kitchen roof, one of our neighbours suggested we contacted a local builder who might be able to help us out. Initially, a quick fix was agreed with a proper repair of the roof scheduled to take place over the summer months.

In those early days, we had a lot of focus and determination to get on with the renovations.

As we started the work, our list of improvements and repairs kept growing longer and longer. Each time we started a job, another issue reared its ugly head and would need to be addressed before we could do the job we had set out to do.

Rather than enjoying the process of renovating the cottage, we started to resent it, it became a chore, and an unpleasant one at that. We started looking for excuses not to crack on with the work. We allowed ourselves to be distracted by other things, and we completely lost focus. The renovations stalled.

And nothing was getting done, that was until late autumn time.

It was a cold and miserable day and we decided to light the wood burner in the lounge. All seemed well at the beginning, but before long we started to smell smoke and our eyes were beginning to sting.

Something was wrong.

Paul, my husband, went upstairs to discover thick swirls of smoke clinging to the ceilings, his eyes burning and gasping for breath, he quickly ran downstairs again shouting: "Put the fire out!". We managed to douse the fire quickly.

Thank goodness the only visible damage we had suffered was some minor smoke damage in the upstairs bedroom. We figured that there must be something wrong with either the wood burner or the chimney. We contacted a chimney repair company the next day.

Even though we were once again presented with an unexpected big bill, it did serve to remind us that we needed to knuckle down and get back to the renovations. This unpleasant incident refocused us.

The renovations resumed and have been in full swing ever since. All the big jobs have now been completed, and we have finally started to decorate.

Dog training can have similar problems and pitfalls.

The Corner Stone Of Dog Training

We need focus, and not just from our dogs. We need to focus on teaching our dogs the skills they need to learn. Focus is something we all need to master.

The ability to focus and concentrate on the job at hand is crucial if we want our dogs to learn, just as our dogs need to focus on us to be able to learn the skills, tasks and behaviours we are trying to teach them. We need to be focused on finding the best way to communicate with them, allowing us to set them up for success.

Having a dog that is focused and listens to you, regardless of the many distractions around, is a joy to own. A dog that loves and enjoys walking with you as much as you enjoy and love walking with them, is one of the reasons most of us get a dog in the first place.

When your dog is struggling to focus on anything but the scents of the rabbits, the pheasants and the hedgerows, it's easy to see why so many dog owners struggle. At that moment you simply don't exist to your dog. Our task is to teach her to pay attention to you regardless of the distractions in the environment around you.

The ultimate goal is to teach your dog to focus on YOU.

Now, it is essential to understand that there are two forms of focus and you need to know what these two forms of focus actually mean.

Focus can either be Forward Focus or Close Focus.

Forward Focus

Forward focus is used when we teach our dogs to do Agility, to retrieve an article or even when we teach them to follow a scent in scent work training. In these circumstances we want our dogs to concentrate on the next jump or retrieving that article or following that scent.

This is precisely the type of focus that inadvertently develops with dogs that pull on the lead. The highly concentrated forward focus of a dog anticipating the excitement of being let off the lead as soon as they reach the park is a challenge to deal with. One that needs to be tackled by changing our dog's expectations when we go for a walk.

Close Focus

The type of focus we want and need from your dog is Close Focus.

Close Focus simply means that your dog's focus is on you, rather than on whatever is going on in the environment around you. An excellent example of close focus is the obedience heel work exercise.

If you have ever watched an obedience competition, you will have seen the level of focus that an obedience dog displays. Their heads are virtually touching their handler's leg, and the dog's gaze is upwards, instead of looking where they are going.

This is Close Focus taken to the extreme and is not the level of focus that you would usually need. It is great for competitions, but I am sure you wouldn't want your dog so focused on you that she walks into lamp posts and pillar boxes.

The Close Focus we are looking for is one that enables your dog to walk on a nice loose lead. You don't need to go so far as to insist that your dog gazes up at you intently.

You can allow your dog to watch where she is going while still paying attention to what you are doing. When taught correctly this will result in a dog that walks nicely beside you on a lovely loose lead.

In order for your dog to want to pay attention to you, we need to make sure that you are more exciting and rewarding that the distractions in the environment around you. You need to be exciting enough to make your dog want to check in with you and give you her attention.

In a perfect world without distractions, our dogs would all quite happily walk next to us on a loose lead. However, we do not live in an ideal world, and there are many distractions on your daily walk that influence your dogs' ability to offer us close focus.

Summary

Dog training requires focus from you, the handler, as well as from your dog.

There are 2 types of focus: Close Focus and Forward Focus.

Forward focus is useful for several popular dog sports, but it is not what we need from your pet dog when you are teaching her not to pull on the lead.

Close Focus is what you need to teach your dog for loose lead walking.

Action Point:

Teaching your dog a nose touch is a great way to teach her amazing skills like Focus, Closeness and Perseverance. A nose touch is where you are asking your dog to bump their nose against your hand.

By My Side

Do you have a dog that loves being by your side and staying with you?

When teaching your dog not to pull on the lead, this is one of the most essential skills to teach her.

The one thing dog owners want from their dogs is for them not to pull on the lead. Sadly most dog owners, and indeed dog trainers, don't realise that teaching a dog to love being close to you is crucial in achieving this goal.

Let me explain by sharing a typical case history with you that illustrates some of the issues that are common to the struggles faced by owners of dogs that pull.

Teaching Tug

Tug simply loves the outdoors; he eagerly explores the hedgerows, hunting out scents across fields and forests. He lives purely for chasing rabbits and, like any typical springer spaniel, springing through the long meadow grass.

Whenever Tug's owner, Mary, takes him for a walk he acts like a coiled spring. Ecstatic about the impending prospect of adventure, causes him to pull like a train.

He is not a big boy, but he's a strong one none-the-less.

Unfortunately, Mary suffers from a bad back and Tug pulling on the lead is a massive issue for her. After each walk she comes back with sore shoulders. Plus, she swears her arms are stretched several inches longer every time she takes Tug out.

Over the past few years, Mary has tried several different things to stop him from pulling.

First she tried a slip lead, which nearly strangled him as he just kept pulling despite the apparent discomfort.

Next she tried a harness that was designed to stop dogs from pulling. It used cords that sit just behind the dog's armpits which tighten each time he starts to pull, making it uncomfortable for him to do so. That so-called "No Pull" harness worked for maybe for 2 walks before Tug learnt to pull again. The main problem with this harness was that because of Tug's continuous pulling it rubbed his armpits raw.

So, it was back to the drawing board.

Next, a head collar was purchased, and Tug hated it. He spent the entire time trying to get the darned thing off! To be fair, it did stop him from pulling. But, he was so miserable wearing it, that he refused to walk at all. Again, this was not a method that worked for Tug.

Ready to give up on Tug ever walking nicely on a lead, she stumbled across my advert in the local paper. In a last-ditch attempt to sort Tug's pulling on the lead, she decided to ask me for some help. She hoped I would be able to offer some advice that would result in some relief from the physical discomfort that walking him caused her, and that I would be able to bring some joy back into their walks together.

When I first met Mary, she was desperate, the chronic pain in her back, the sore shoulders and arms, were really getting too much to bear.

Walking Tug had become a chore rather than a fun way to enjoy each other's company and the beautiful countryside she lived in. She told me she had tried everything and that nothing worked. After spending a few minutes with them, I quickly identified that there was one key piece of the puzzle missing in their relationship.

To Mary, teaching a dog to walk on a nice loose lead was as simple as putting a lead on her dog and going for a walk. One of her first mistakes was that every time she had tried a new piece of dog training equipment like the harness or head collar, she had merely slapped it on him and gone for a walk. She had failed to actually teach Tug to walk on any of the training aids before attempting to take him out.

What she hadn't realised was that teaching a dog to walk on a nice loose lead is more than just putting a dog into a piece of equipment that promises to solve all your lead walking and dog training struggles.

You see, she never ever, in all that she tried, actually tried to teach Tug to walk by her side. She just assumed that he would want to please her and do it.

She assumed that Tug would want to walk with her simply because he loves her. She did not believe that giving him rewards for staying by her side would solve the problem she was having.

She voiced her concern to me when she asked me: "But what happens when I eventually stop using these treats? Will he revert to pulling on the lead? I don't want to have to bribe him by offering treats all the time."

Those concerns are probably the ones swirling around your head too.

I don't blame you. The original reward-based training methods to teach a dog to walk next to us relied on the dog staying by your side because you are holding a treat in your hand. Leading the dog much like a donkey walking forwards when a carrot is dangled in front of him on a stick. The trouble comes when it is time to phase out the rewards. This is where a lot of dog owners fail.

Reducing the use of rewards in dog training is not as simple as it seems. It requires a reduction in the rewards carried out in such a way that it keeps dogs gambling on when the next reward is coming. And this process requires a skill level that is beyond that of the average pet dog owner.

The other problem with using this method to teach your dog to walk on a loose lead is that most people find that the dog will focus on them when there are few distractions, but many dogs do not think it is advantageous to stay by our side when there are exciting bunny smells in the long grass, or when there are other dogs to go say "Hi" to.

There is something missing and that is a genuine desire on our dog's part to stay with us in the face of all these overwhelming distractions.

Tug's owner simply was not interesting enough for him to want to be with her. He had no reason to stay close to his owner as it wasn't where the fun in his walk came from. The joy in Tug's walk came from the distractions all around him. This was aided by the fact that his owner paid him little attention on their walks. She allowed him to be distracted by the environment.

Staying Close

In an ideal situation, we would start to convince a young puppy that the simple act of being near us is fun and rewarding. Even before we clip on the lead for the first time. If we do this, then teaching her to walk on a loose lead will be a lot easier because she will actually want to be near us.

This is precisely the approach we need to take when teaching the life skill I call Closeness.

Closeness is creating and nurturing the desire for our dogs to want to stay with us, no matter what.

Creating this desire in Tug was the first step to improving the relationship between him and his owner. But developing this one aspect of teaching him to walk by his owner's side didn't stop Tug from pulling on the lead.

For that, we needed some other skills too. Let's hop over to the next chapter and have a look at one of the most important things we should teach every dog right from the start.

Summary

Teaching your dog to want to be close to you at home as well as out and about is an important skill to teach her.

While there are different equipment options available to you, such as head collars and harnesses, you still need to teach your dog to walk on a loose lead. If you fail to do this, your dog will definitely learn to pull.

You need to become the most important person and fun thing ever to your dog.

You always need to remember to pay attention to your dog, regardless of what is going on around you.

Action Point:

Reward your dog with a treat or a game for wanting to be close to you.

You can even encourage your dog to climb all over you, putting their paws on your feet or lap, touching your legs with her shoulder or even pushing her head in between your legs.

Reward her for doing this with treats or with an interactive game of gentle tug.

To Have Or Not To Have

Unlike Shakespeare's Hamlet where the phrase "To Be or Not to Be" was first coined, "To Have or Not to Have" has nothing to do with the story of Hamlet descending into "feigned" madness by the need for revenge on his uncle for murdering his father, the King of Denmark, who appears to him as a ghost.

Instead, I am referring to the importance of being able to control your impulses, and in this chapter, we are going to be exploring self-control and its uses in dog training.

Self-control is a vital skill to learn.

You see, self-control determines how we are going to behave in everyday life. It doesn't govern all the choices we make during our day, but it influences a fair few of them.

Self-control stops you from buying that fancy new sports car when you haven't got the funds to pay for it. It prevents you from having that second helping of dessert or buying cakes in the supermarket when you are trying to lose weight.

Let me share with you one of my biggest weaknesses.

I cannot deny it, but one of my biggest weaknesses is my love for chocolate. To me chocolate is like a best friend, it is what gets me through the day.

I admit it, I am a chocoholic. I just cannot live without chocolate in my life.

I imagine you are all snug and curled up in your most comfy favourite chair wondering how the heck my love of chocolate has anything to do with dog training. Well, the way I see it, a lot, actually.

The Marshmallow Test

Have ever heard of the Marshmallow test?

Back in the early 60's Walter Mischel and his graduate students started an experiment at the Stanford University Bing's Nursery School, this experiment would become known as The Marshmallow Test.

Imagine this scene: A nursery school child, sitting at a table. A delicate plate on which a fluffy and decadent marshmallow rests. The child's face contorted in concentration, squirming on his chair trying to resist the temptation to grab and stuff the marshmallow into his mouth…

The experiment was simple in its brilliance. The children were given a simple choice, they could eat the marshmallow now or wait alone for up to 20 minutes for the researchers to bring them the bigger reward of an extra marshmallow on their return.

Years later the team went back and the pre-schoolers who had waited for the second bigger reward had fared better in life than the ones who had eaten the one marshmallow when it was offered. They had developed better self-control.

Over the years since, this test has become the measuring stick by which willpower aka self-control, temptation and determination are defined.

I can tell you now that if you were to do this test on me today, leaving me with a plate with delicious chocolate resting on it, and the sweet scent of chocolate heavy in the air, I am not sure if I could resist and wait for you to return with another.

Would you be able to leave the chocolate and not have a sneaky taste? Perhaps you would resort to licking the chocolate to get a little of the flavour without actually eating it?

It all depends on how big your desire for that chocolate is, right?

If you are like me and love chocolate, then you are very likely to give in to temptation and eat the chocolate before too long. It would take me a large amount of self-control to force myself not to eat it.

Now if I were to replace that chocolate for a tube of mints, would that make a difference to your response?

Would your level of desire for the mints be as strong as your desire for the chocolates?

For me the mints would quite easily stay there until the end of time. Because I simply don't like them, I don't desire them. I don't need self-control around the mints, but with the chocolates, it is a whole different story.

I really need to stop myself from eating the chocolate as I love it so. This means I must use self-control.

Self-Control And Choices

Now let's go back to our dogs. They need to learn self-control too.

Self-control is very closely linked to focus and determination.

But what does self-control actually mean and how do we teach it to our dogs?

Self-control is when your dog makes a choice not to chase or pick up that half rotting sandwich from the road. It is your dog choosing to stay with you, even if she is surrounded by exciting distractions.

When we talk about self-control in dog training, we are looking for dogs to choose us over the distractions in the environment. It means that we do not always have to tell them "No", "Don't Do That" or "Leave it". Self-control allows our dogs to make the right choices in life.

However, for you to be able to teach your dog self-control, we need to create desire, because if she has no desire, she will feel no need for restraint. We need to use something that your dog loves to play with or even eat to build that desire so that you can then use this to teach your dog the willpower she needs.

Your dog needs to learn to display a level of self-control, without you, the owner, having to continually remind her to stay with you and ignore that rabbit, pheasant, deer or any smells, sights and sounds that might take her attention away.

Self-Control is one of those really challenging life skills, one where you have to trust your dog to make the right choice. And it really is all about choices. Just like us humans make dozens, if not hundreds, of decisions every single day dogs are faced with choices too. What we want to do when teaching Self Control is to shape your dog's choices so that she makes the choice that you want her to make.

To do this, you need to make the right choices more rewarding than the wrong ones. This in no way means that you should punish your dog for making the wrong choice. Instead, you should make the right decision so tempting that your dog will not contemplate making any other choice.

This whole concept might become a little clearer if I give you an example of how this would work in a real-life situation.

Let's pretend your dog loves to chase rabbits.

To your dog, chasing rabbits is the bee's knees and the one thing your dog loves to do more than anything else in the world. As soon as the scent of rabbits wafts across your dog's nose she forgets about anything else except that she wants no, needs, to chase that rabbit.

She just adores the thrill of the chase. It doesn't matter whether she catches the rabbit; the pursuit in itself is rewarding enough for her to want to repeat this behaviour over and over again.

As an animal lover, you don't like the fact that your dog is so obsessed with chasing rabbits. You need to find a way to stop this.

The other challenge you have is that chasing can very rapidly become a habit and this behaviour can generalise to chasing other things such as other dogs, cyclists, runners or cars. It becomes vitally important that you stop your dog from practising this chasing behaviour.

One way you can do this is through management, by keeping your dog on a lead or a long line in the presence of rabbits so you can stop her from chasing and prevent her from practising the unwanted behaviour.

The big problem with this approach is that she will never learn not to chase rabbits. So instead of just managing your dog's behaviour, you also need to actively encourage her to make the right choices.

By making those right choices more rewarding for your dog than the enjoyment she gets out of chasing rabbits, you will be able to start changing her behaviour to the response you want.

You need to change her perspective on what is the more rewarding behaviour. The end result you are looking for is that your dog will put more value in staying with you than chasing after the rabbits.

While we can prevent your dog from making the wrong choices, managing the situation is not a valid long-term strategy. So, although management can play an essential role in stopping your dog from making the wrong choices, it's better if we teach your dog an alternative behaviour by making the alternative more appealing.

This results in your dog choosing the new behaviour and the choice we prefer when we take away the management strategies.

This approach will prevent your dog from reverting to the previous preferred behaviour of chasing the rabbits.

Summary

Your dog makes many different choices on a daily basis and some of these choices are aligned with what we want from our dogs, while others are undesirable to us.

By making the undesirable choices less accessible and attractive, we can influence our dogs and start to promote self-control and grow the desire for the choices we want her to make.

Management is a tool but not a viable long-term strategy.

Self-control means that your dog is making the right choices without us having to nag her to do so.

Action Point:

An easy way to start teaching your dog to make the right choices in life is to watch your dog and every time she does something you like, even though you haven't asked for it, reward her.

Remember: These are choices that your dog has made. If we reward the choices we like, your dog will start making that choice more often because it is now more rewarding for her to do so.

The Good, The Bad And The Ugly

I don't know whether you will remember but back in the sixties, there was a movie that bore this name. It became a very famous Spaghetti Western starring Clint Eastwood, though it is not my intention to talk about this movie here.

No... the Good, the Bad and the Ugly we are talking about here has nothing to do with a bounty hunting gunslinger or a criminal trying initially to kill the gunslinger. Nor has it anything to do with a sadistic, psychopathic enemy, the Union Army or even buried treasure worth a mind boggling (in Wild West times) $20,000.

Or has it?

In a way the mechanics of how excitement (which is also known as "Arousal" in behavioural science's terms) builds in your dog's brain and the dynamics between the 3 main characters of that film do have similarities.

You see the Gunslinger is the Good guy, he embodies the Good of excitement.
The second criminal is the Bad guy. He will cross the line but still has some honour which has him teaming up with the good guy at a crucial point in the story. This is like Bad Excitement,

where your ability to make rational decisions is compromised but not completely gone out of the window.

The Sadistic psychopath, who the gunslinger and the criminal team up to beat, is the Ugly. Really Ugly! This is like the Ugly Excitement where no rational thought can be processed and as a result, bad and inappropriate decisions are made.

Excitement and how it builds and controls your dog's behaviour involves a really complex process which is fuelled by the production of certain hormones and the interaction between those hormones in your dog's brain.

I could go on to explain which hormones and which area of the brain is involved, but you would be fast asleep by the time I finish typing the first sentence, so I am not going to go there. No sane, none geeky, normal person would find this stuff that interesting anyway. If you do, there are plenty of other books that will cover that detail for you.

I will say though, that in very simple terms, excitement determines how your dog will respond in different situations and encounters with other dogs and people.

What we want to teach our dogs is to be able to think even if they are getting excited and fired up about something. We want them to be able to think things through before deciding how they are going to respond, and then make a good choice. A choice that does not involve becoming reactive, but one that will diffuse the situation and allow their excitement levels to calm back down to a healthy level.

This really is an important life skill to teach your dog.

The topic of Excitement is complicated so let me try and see if I can make it a little clearer.

Your dog's excitement level will determine whether your dog is able to respond to you and the environment in the way we want them to. If your dog's excitement levels are too high, she will start to make bad choices and start reacting negatively to the situation she finds herself in.

We need to find a way to keep the excitement at a manageable level.

Let's have a look at some different examples to explain the good, the bad and the ugly of excitement. Hopefully, this will help you to begin to understand how excitement works.

For our dogs to be able to learn we need a certain amount of excitement to improve their learning and performance level, especially when your dog competes in agility, flyball or obedience.

We also need a certain amount of excitement in our dogs to enable them to be competitive. With pet dogs, for example, this will give us a dog that is able to respond immediately to a recall no matter what the distractions are. This is the good excitement.

But where there is Good excitement there is also Bad excitement. This happens when a dog becomes over excited and his ability to respond to our cues and requests decreases. This then results in a dog that is less careful in the choices she makes and as a result starts to make the wrong ones. These choices may lead to your dog knocking down a pole in an agility competition, in flyball, it might lead to her not catching the ball or dropping it on the return leg of her run and in obedience it will lead to missing cues.

In pet dogs, this kind of excitement is likely to result in pulling on the lead or their noses being glued to the floor as you are walking them.

Then we also have the downright Ugly end of the excitement scale. This is where the dog's excitement level is so high that she is no longer able to respond to our requests at all. Dogs that are over-excited consistently make the wrong choices. They are unable to see the correct choices even if we present them on a gold platter.

A dog that has become extremely reactive to her environment is a dog that is over-excited or over-aroused. This is the dog that is screaming, barking and lunging at the end of the lead. The dog that bites and attacks another dog on a walk.

Let me give you a few real-life examples that will hopefully make this whole arousal thing a little clearer.

Good Excitement

You have been for a very relaxing walk with your dog. On your way home you pass a house, and there is a big Labrador in the front garden, standing by the gate barking at you.

Your dog calmly walks past barely sparing a glance towards the barking Labrador.

In this scenario, your dog's arousal levels are such that she can cope with the situation, making the correct response and staying attentive to you the whole time.

Bad Excitement

Let us take the same walk again.

However, this time a cat jumps out at you both. Hissing and lashing out before running off at high speed and disappearing into the scrubs at the side of the road.

Your dog copes ok with this event. Maybe she glances and glares at the cat, but without reacting in an outright negative way to its presence. However, the excitement level is starting to build.

You carry on walking and continue past the house with the barking Labrador.

This time your dog glances uncertainly at the barking hound and starts pulling on the lead, to try and walk past more quickly.

This time your dog's arousal levels are raised, and she is starting to make the wrong choices.

The wrong choice here is pulling you past the house.

And Then There Is The Ugly Excitement

The next day we go on the same walk but this time your dog sees a rabbit to chase and the cat jumps out at you both, hissing and lashing out before running off at high speed and disappearing into the scrubs at the side of the road again. You pass gardens where kids are playing, running around and shouting.

You keep going, and again you walk past the house with the big barking Labrador standing at the front gate as you go past.

This time your dog reacts badly, she barks back. Pulls on the lead towards the gate and is a real handful. You struggle to control her, the Labrador in the garden increases his show of aggression and things quickly escalate.

You are now left to drag away a snarling mess of a dog that keeps spinning around, and it takes you to the end of the long road before you get any semblance of control back.

The difference between our first walk and this third walk is that, this time, there have been several incidents and occurrences that have one after the other continually raised your dog's excitement level.

By the time you got to the garden with the barking Labrador, your dog's excitement level was so high that she was no longer able to think rationally about whether or not the barking dog in the garden was a threat. Your dog acted on instinct alone and reacted badly to the whole situation.

For your dog to be able to behave the way you want her to, we need to teach your dog to return to a calm state between exciting incidents.

By teaching our dog the life skill to "Think When Excited" we are developing her ability to think and learn as excitement levels increase, making it less likely that she will choose the wrong response in any given situation.

Some examples of how teaching your dog to think when excited will help you and your dog are:

Before:

Your dog is able to walk on a nice loose lead in your house and garden and perhaps during dog training lessons in the local hall, but when you are out walking along the road on the way to the local park, there is no way your dog will walk nicely on a loose lead.

After:

Your dog is now able to walk on a nice loose lead no matter where you are. Even in new environments your dog stays focused on you and responds to your request to heel instantly, just like she does at home or training class.

Before:

Your dog is slow, distracted and sloppy whenever you ask her to perform a behaviour; such as a sit or down etc.

After:

Your dog can do snappy sits and downs when asked.

Summary

Your dog's excitement level will determine how receptive she will be to your requests and instructions.

A little excitement is good. It allows your dog to respond quickly to your instructions. As your dog's excitement level rises, she will be less responsive to you.

When your dog gets overexcited, she will not be able to think rationally or make the right choices.

Teaching your dog to think when excited and to calm down quickly after an event will help her to be able to respond to your requests and make the right decisions.

Action Point:

An easy exercise to start teaching your dog to calm down after excitement is to first raise the excitement levels by asking her to do a series of four or five doggy push-ups one after the other in quick succession. Doggy push-ups are quick sit-down-sits done as a fluid movement. Then calming the excitement down by asking for a minute down-stay.

By combining high excitement exercises with calming exercises you will teach your dog to switch more easily between high and low excitement levels.

Keep Calm

Have you ever been so excited that you just could not stand still, that you had to run from pillar to post in anticipation?

Too excited to sleep, you toss and turn all night long because you know the morning will bring the much-anticipated change, opportunity, holiday or… (you can fill in your own thing here)?

Or maybe you have received an unexpected gift, and you are so excited that you cannot wait to tear the wrapping paper off it?

I definitely have been that excited.

A Dream Came True

I think I might have mentioned that I love animals and was majorly into horses as a young girl.

After the disappearing act that I pulled to be with the horses, their owner persuaded my parents to allow me to take riding lessons at the local riding school.

MEGA Squeal!
If I was that mad on horses and wanted to be around them, she suggested, the safest thing to do was to make sure I learnt how

to take care of them properly and learnt how to stay safe at the same time.

It was a good argument, and my parents agreed.

I can tell you, I was over the moon! So excited that I woke up extra early on that much anticipated day. My dreams of riding a horse would finally come true. I raced around the house pulling open all the curtains, waking up the household. I think I might even have shrieked at the top of my voice. It was all a bit much for my mum, so rudely woken at the crack of dawn by an over-excited child.

My excitement level was off the charts. Uncontrollable and way over the top. Especially considering the lesson wasn't until late afternoon. I was told in a firm voice to get a hold of myself, be patient and calm down. I was even given the added task of 'go and tidy your room'.

My mum knew that if I stayed that excited for the entire day, things would not end well.

She made sure that I calmed down so that I would be able to enjoy the experience, and ultimately, be able to learn to ride a horse.

Growing Calmness

Things are the same for our dogs. If they are too excited to go for a walk, they will make bad decisions and will not be able to learn those things that we want them to learn and won't really enjoy the experience of going for a walk.

Keeping your dog calm is actually an essential skill for her to learn, even when we are teaching your dog not to pull.

Calm dogs will be less likely to react to distractions like scents carried on the air, rustlings in the hedgerows, cyclists racing by or other people out walking their dogs.

Dogs that are on edge or excited will be actively looking and searching for things to chase and explore.

Although it might seem teaching a dog to be calm will be counterintuitive to having any effect on her ability to walk on a nice loose lead, it is well worth spending time and effort to create a confident, calm and relaxed dog.

A common reason for dogs being reactive on a lead is that they are way too hyped up by the process of getting ready for a walk to be able to make good choices when we take them out.

Removing some of the things that tell your dog that something exciting is just about to happen, like putting on your coat or getting the lead out, will already go a long way to ensuring she is in the right frame of mind before you go out on a walk.

You can take some simple steps to ensure that your dog no longer sees these things as signs that something exciting is about to happen. Often, something as simple as putting your shoes on way before it is time to go for a walk and then just going about your daily business, will help stop her from becoming overly excited about going out.

Summary

Being calm and relaxed is an important skill to teach your dog.

One of the leading causes for reactivity is too high an excitement level for the situation.

Harnessing the power of being calm will prevent your dog from making the wrong choices. So, it is essential to make sure your dog is calm and in the right frame of mind before going out for a walk.

Simple things like putting your keys in your pocket or putting your shoes on way before you intend to go out can help keep your dog calmer.

Action Point:

Watch your dog and notice when she is being calm and relaxed. Maybe she is laying down on the floor or in her bed.

Reward her for relaxing by placing a treat next to her when she is settled in her bed or on the floor. Can she stay calm and relaxed after eating her treat?

Yes? Go back and again, place a treat next to her.

No? Wait for your dog to calm down and relax again. Then go back and place a treat next to her.

Bouncebackability: The Power Of Adaptability

When I first started to write this chapter, I was thinking of calling it Flexibility. Then I realised you might end up with visions of you and your dog stretching your muscles, lengthening your spine or even doing Yoga together. That is not the type of Flexibility I was going for, so I decided to call this chapter Bouncebackability: The Power of Adaptability instead.

Although, if all that stretching, lengthening your spine and balancing on balls floats your boat then Doggy Yoga or perhaps DOBO is something you should check out. Dogs are incredible and amazing animals that can learn to do the most amazing stuff!

Anyway, your dog's ability to bounce back is an important one. Let me explain.

Learning To Walk

Remember when you first learnt to walk and then run? I bet you had a few wobbles and you probably fell down more times than you can remember, though I suppose it would be more correct to say that you fell over more time than your parents can remember.

The crucial thing to realise is that each time you fell you got back up and tried again. If you hadn't, you would not be able to walk on 2 legs today.

You bounced back. You adapted your approach. You kept trying, again and again, each time you fell over because you were determined to learn to walk.

This is what the skill of Adaptability is all about. It is about not giving up when things get tough.

I bet you have used the skill of Adaptability time and time again as you grew up. Adapting the way you approach a problem until you find a way that works. Even now in your adult life, I guess you are not the kind of person that gives up after just one try. It is human nature to want to succeed in life, no matter what your goal is.

Having the ability to bounce back, to adapt after disappointment, to persevere and to try a different approach, is all part of the skill I like to refer to as "Adaptability".

And this is an essential skill for your dog to learn.

Solving Problems

When you learn to be adaptable, you learn to change little things in the way you approach a problem. You learn that if one way of doing something doesn't work and you take a slightly different path, you get closer to your goal. You keep trying and changing little things until you find an approach that works.

After all, as Einstein once said *"Insanity is doing the same thing over and over and expecting a different result"*, there is no point in doing the same thing repeatedly so you keep on failing.

The key to being adaptable is working your way through and trying different things until you find the ones that work for you. And this is precisely what we need your dog to learn.

Your dog needs to learn to be adaptable and try different things when confronted with a challenge. She needs to learn to change her approach to fit each new situation.

If your dog is one that loves to chase rabbits, then each time she smells a rabbit, it will be difficult for her to stay with you. Her instinct will be telling her that she needs to follow that scent, chase and hunt down the rabbit. Until you teach your dog the skill of Adaptability, she simply does not have any clue that there is a different response that she can use in those situations.

By teaching your dog the skill of being flexible in the way she responds, we can prepare her to adapt and learn to react in several different ways to the same or a similar situation.

This means that instead of having a single response when she comes across the scent of a rabbit, we can now teach her several different answers to choose from in the same situation. This means that we can help her make the right choice. The choice that we want is for her not to pull on the lead in an attempt to follow that scent.

Instead of pulling on the lead, when for example another dog approaches, we now get a dog that is calm, able to respond to us and ignore the dog coming towards her. Of course, teaching this skill is not something that we can do overnight. As we train your dog to adapt and be more flexible in her responses, you will start to see a marked improvement in your dog's behaviour, and over time she will learn to make the correct choice in similar situations.

Summary

As we grow up, we learn to adapt physically as well as mentally. We learn to approach problems from different angles and this helps us succeed and reach our goals.

Your dog needs to learn this same skill.

Dogs that can adapt and be flexible in their responses tend to be calmer and more responsive to their owners.

A dog that can be flexible and offer different responses in the same situation will be better prepared for life within our human society.

Action Point:

Observe your dog and see if you can figure out if she always reacts in the same way in the same or similar situations. If she does, try and get her to do something different.

For example: if your dog always rushes to the door as soon as you go to open it, ask her to do a sit by the door instead.

Then next time you go to the door ask her to do a down.

Power Of Rewards

It is a simple, but well-known fact in the dog training world, that dogs will do what is good for them.

They do what is rewarding to them.

It's All In The Reward

We really can't have a chapter about rewards and how responsive your dog is to the rewards on offer, without making it abundantly clear that dogs will do what is rewarding to them.

It is the first rule of dog training.

The trouble is that what your dog finds rewarding is not the same as what we think she finds rewarding.

What gets rewarded gets repeated.

This is the first law of how dogs learn. However, the second law of dog training is just as significant as the first one, and that law is:

Rewards need to be rewarding.

You might think that it is enough to praise your dog by telling her "Good Girl" or "Clever Girl".

However, when you are saying that, your dog will be thinking: "that is all well and good and extremely nice of you to say so... But that scent over there is mighty interesting". Before you know it, she will be pulling you off your feet and ignoring your pleas to come back to heel, rather following the scent that has piqued her interest.

The rewards that you offer your dog for doing the things you want her to do, like walking nicely on a loose lead, must be exciting enough to convince her that the better deal is to stay with you.

You need to find that one thing that your dog values above all else.

The reward you choose to use must be appealing enough to stop her pulling on the lead as soon as an intoxicating smell wafts across her nose or a leaf tumbles and dances in the wind catching her attention.

It sounds so easy when dog trainers tell you to use a treat to reward your dog for doing something right.

The truth though is that using rewards when training your dog is not as simple as it first appears.

Yes, it is true that in an ideal world we reward the dog for making the right choices. However, your dog's ability to respond to the rewards we are offering depends on a lot of different things.

Why Won't My Dog Take Treats?

The first thing you must evaluate is whether your dog is in the right frame of mind to be able to take the rewards on offer.

For example; if your dog gets scared by a loud bang, she will be unable to play with a toy or even eat a treat. Emotionally she will be preparing to flee. When you are running for your life, you do not need your digestive system. All the energy that would typically go into digesting food is now being diverted to her muscles to allow her to get away faster.

This means that a scared dog is physically unable to take or eat treats.

Finding The Magic Reward

Secondly, if the reward you are offering your dog doesn't trump the reward she is getting from following her instinct, then she will do what she finds more rewarding, ignoring any instructions coming from you.

Let's assume your dog's ultimate reward is following rabbit scents. Your dog typically loves treats. However, you have tried all sorts of different food rewards and, in this situation, food is not what she wants. No amount of cut up roast beef is going to distract her from her primary focus: following that scent.

You need to get creative.

Let's pretend we can bottle the scent of the rabbits and infuse her favourite toy with it. We could then use this toy with its tantalising rabbit scent to reward her for making the right choice.

Now wouldn't that be fabulous?

Luckily for us, toys exist that are made from rabbit skin, these toys tend to be irresistible to dogs who love to follow rabbit scents.

So, if your dog loves rabbit scents, then you can use a toy like this to reward her with a quick game of tug or chase-the-toy every time she gives us a split second of attention.

Over time those glimpses of attention will become a few seconds of focus, and it won't be long before you are able to ask for longer and longer moments of concentration — one thing we need to bear in mind though is that we must start teaching this away from distractions.

The above is an example of how you can use the one thing that your dog desires above all else and turn it into a reward for her making the right choice.

You will need to put in some work to identify that one thing that your dog will do anything for. Every dog is different!

Turning Distractions Into Successes

Thirdly, the number of distractions there are in the area where you are walking, training and playing with your dog is another crucial thing to consider.

When you first start working on any struggle you need to carefully manage the level of distraction present when you train your dog.

By starting with the lowest level of distraction possible, you will be setting your dog up for success.

Instead of starting a new exercise in the park, at the beach or in the woods, you need to start each new game or exercise in a quiet room in your home. Once your dog has learnt what is required and "got it", you can then move to a different place with a few more distractions going on.

By slowly building up the level of distractions you will be able to make sure that your dog succeeds every step of the way. Once she has mastered the game in the home, you can take her into the back garden. Again, going back to basics and working your way through the steps of the exercise until your dog "gets it" in this new environment.

By gradually increasing the level of distractions we can make sure that your dog succeeds at each stage. From the back garden we might progress to the front yard, then to the little grassy square at the end of your road etc.

The other thing to remember is that as the level of distraction in the environment increases you also need to use higher value rewards to keep your dog engaged with you.

Using Low And High-Value Rewards

At home, you will be able to use a portion of your dog's regular food as the reward, but as you move to other areas, you will need to switch to using higher value rewards to maintain the same level of engagement and response from her.

Talking about rewards, there is one other thing we need to consider, and that is how to deliver the rewards. What I mean by this is that there is more to reward based training than just shoving the food into your dog's mouth and watching her eat it!

The way you present the reward, and the speed with which you do so, also has a significant impact on what your dog is learning. Sometimes you will need to do rapid-fire the rewards straight into your dog's mouth; creating more excitement and more engagement with you.

At other times, for example, when you are looking for calmness, it is better to slow down the delivery of the reward in such a way that the anticipation of the food's arrival gives you the quietness and stillness that you are looking for.

Even the placement of the reward onto a blanket or bed can help convey the right message to your dog. For example, when you are playing bed games, you want your dog to value the bed so by placing the rewards on the bed, rather than delivering the food directly to your dog's mouth, you are helping her to calm down.

Summary

Behaviours that get rewarded get repeated.

The rewards you use need to be rewarding for your dog.

Identify the foods and toys that your dog loves and use those as rewards.

Use low-value rewards when there are few distractions, and higher value rewards when there are more distractions.

When teaching a new behaviour, slowly increase the level of distractions.

How you deliver your rewards is just as important as the rewards themselves.

Action Point:

Next time you go out to walk your dog try taking a variety of treats. Make sure you have lower and higher value rewards in the mix.

Use the lower value treats to reward your dog when there are no distractions and the high value rewards when the distractions are greater.

Experiment with how you deliver your treats. Quick rewards for quick responses. Slow rewards when you want your dog to calm down.

5 Steps To Becoming A Model Walking Companion

Have you ever tried to learn a new skill?

It doesn't matter whether the new skill you are trying to learn is a language or whether you are trying to learn to play a musical instrument. Looking at learning the skill as a whole can be a daunting prospect.

Bite Sized Learning

Whether you are successful at learning a new skill depends on how you approach the subject. Jumping in feet first without a real plan of how you are going to learn that new skill rarely works.

Trying to hold a conversation in a new language or playing a complicated piece of music right from the start will most likely lead to failure.

Instead, finding a way to break the task down into easily digestible and achievable chunks will greatly improve your chance of succeeding. We sometimes need to break down those chunks even more, until we get to very small bite, or even nibble, sized pieces.

Last year I started to learn to play the saxophone. I got myself a shiny new sax which was a thing of beauty, gleaming gold-lacquered brass with mother of pearl inlaid keys. There was nothing I wanted to do more than playing a tune on this gorgeous instrument.

Learning to play was not that easy. The first few times I tried to blow on the mouthpiece, all I got was a series of farts!

I kid you not!

The only sound I was able to produce at the beginning sounded a lot more like someone blowing raspberries than anything resembling a musical note.

Luckily, I have a very good mentor, a teacher who helped me break down the task of getting a sound out of the saxophone.

He told me in my first lesson, that there is no way I should expect to be able to get a clear and recognisable note out of that sax if I did not first learn how to put the reed properly onto the mouthpiece. The next thing he told me to do, and this piece of advice was not easy to swallow, was to take the mouthpiece and put the rest of my saxophone back in its case.

I was heartbroken, that gorgeous shiny saxophone was now confined to its sturdy black velvet lined case!

I spent the next hour practising how to blow on the mouthpiece alone. Continuing until I could produce and hold a nice bright note.

Once I had mastered that nice steady note on the mouthpiece alone, he allowed me to attach the neck. Much of the next lesson was spent learning to play and hold that one note steady using just the mouthpiece connected to the saxophone neck. Towards the end of that second lesson, I was finally allowed to fully assemble my saxophone.

At that point, I had become fairly competent at producing the note "C". And that was just the start of my saxophone journey.

I had another huge obstacle to tackle though in my quest to learn to play. I knew nothing about how to read music.

If I am completely honest, that is not completely true. I had a rudimentary understanding of what notes were, and what some of the annotations meant. But I did not know how to relate that information to the instrument I so desperately wanted to learn how to play.

The way I see it, learning to play an instrument is very similar to learning a new language. To enable me to learn I really had to break the whole process down into small bite-sized pieces.

Even when I was ready to start learning to play little tunes on the saxophone, I had to break down each line of the music into its individual bars. Practicing playing each note of the bar in the correct order. Once I mastered that task, I could move on learning to play the next bar before stringing first 2 and then 3 bars together.

I must say my progress was painfully slow to start with but, as time went on, I was able to play the tunes, holding each note for the correct amount of time and at the correct speed.

Do you know what? Training a dog not to pull on the leash is not that different from learning to play the saxophone or learning a new language.

What we need to do is to break down walking on a lead, firstly into its component parts and then break those parts down into bite-sized pieces. Then we can teach our dogs each of these parts through a series of games and exercises.

And this is exactly what we will be doing in this chapter.

Step 1: Getting Ready For Action

I don't know about you but every time I get ready to go out, I go through this little ritual of putting on my boots and coat, picking up the keys, my handbag and everything else I might need when I go out.

I am sure you do the same thing when you get ready to take your dog out for a walk. It's natural we are all creatures of habit and it doesn't matter whether you have been around the block a few times, have a young family, live on your own or you are a college student.

We all have habits, it is perfectly normal to have them and in some ways, these habits help us get through our daily lives. The trouble is though dogs are creatures of habit too. And our "getting ready" routines can lead to problems when our dog starts to predict that this means that she's going out for a walk. The very first thing we tend to do when we are thinking of taking our dog for a walk is probably grabbing our shoes and coat and our dog's lead. It sounds simple, doesn't it?

But you might be surprised to learn that a lot of dogs and owners struggle with this. It is something that can become a huge problem for them when the dog is not comfortable with the equipment being used to take her out.

This feeling of being uncomfortable with the process of putting the lead on for example, can present itself in several different ways. Perhaps your dog starts to run around in what you are assuming are excited circles or she starts to bark. Maybe she runs to her bed and lies down on it, or rolls on her back when the collar and lead come out.

These are all signs that your dog is not comfortable with what is about to happen next.

Your dog is simply not enjoying the experience; she might even be fearful of what is happening and placing the leash on her is simply too much for her to cope with. This can lead to all sorts of problems with your dog, from them shutting down, to displays of extreme excitement like jumping up, spinning on the spot and even biting.

I did a little digging and came across some very interesting statistics:

According to the DogDailyStar.com, a free daily dog magazine website for dog lovers, a staggering 20% of dog bites occur when owners try to put a collar, harness or lead onto their own dog.

Whilst according to the article "Contexts and consequences of dog bite incidents", published in the Journal of Veterinary Behaviour (Volume 23), 76% of the dog bites recorded in their research occurred when the owner bent over the dog.

These statistics clearly indicate that teaching a dog to accept having a collar, harness or head collar put on and a lead attached is something that we all should pay more attention to. We generally just assume that a dog will be okay with having a collar put around her neck, a harness pushed over her head and attached around her body or even a having a head collar plonked on her face. And this is where the problems start.

Instead of just assuming that your dog is okay with this, we need to spend some time making sure that they are happy having a collar, harness, head collar and lead put on.

Harness Shaping

The easiest way to get your dog used to a collar, head collar or harness is to gradually introduce it, making sure that your dog develops a positive association with the piece of equipment that you prefer to use.

For ease of teaching you how to do this I will describe how to teach your dog to accept having a harness put on. Though this exercise can easily be adapted to introduce a collar or head collar.

Step 1:

Hold the harness in your hand and let your dog sniff it.

When she does, tell her how amazing she is and give her a little treat. Repeat this step six or seven times.

Step 2:

Next, hold the harness together so it forms an open loop. Let your dog sniff it. Tell her how great she is and reward with a little treat.

Keep repeating this step until your dog comes forwards calmly as soon as you present the harness.

Step 3:

Once your dog is happily coming forwards, start asking her to put her head through the harness.

Keep rewarding each attempt she makes to put her head through the gap.

Step 4:

Now switch to holding the harness the same way you would when you are about to put it on your dog.

Make sure to keep the head loop as open as possible.

Again, ask your dog to put her head through the loop. Reward her when she does. Repeat 6 or 7 times until your dog is happily and confidently putting her head through the loop.

Step 5:

You are now ready to slip the harness over your dog's head as she puts it through the head loop.

Remember to reward your dog.

Repeat this step 6 or 7 times, until your dog is completely happy with this step.

Step 6

Once the harness is over your dog's head, lower it so it gently rests on her shoulders.

Tell your dog what a good girl she is and Reward.

Repeat this step 6 or 7 times until she is completely happy with it.

Step 7:

Fasten the harness. Tell your dog how amazing she is and reward her.

I cover this whole process in detail on the "No Pulling Allowed" online mini course that comes as a bonus with this book (For full details please visit:
www. nopullingallowed.co.uk/bookbonuses).

Once you have taught your dog to accept and actively love having her harness and lead put on, we are ready to consider taking her for a walk, but before we leave the house, we need to make sure that she is calm and collected.

This neatly leads us to our second step.

Step 2: Controlling The Excitement Before Going Out

Controlling the excitement before you go out for a walk might seem a silly thing to suggest. Of course, your dog is excited to go out for her walk! You would probably be surprised and perhaps even a little worried if your dog did not show any excitement when a walk was offered.

However, the level of excitement that your dog shows has a direct impact on how she is going to behave on the walk. The calmer your dog is when you start the walk, the less likely she is to rush out of the door and pull when on your walk. The calmer your dog the more controlled the walk will be.

Consider the following scenario:

Your dog is excitedly jumping up and down, barking and nipping your hands when you are attempting to put your shoes on, bending down to do the laces up on your shoes is a challenge as you are trying to avoid being nipped in the face as you bend down. You try and tell your dog to calm down, but she is just getting more and more excited.

Next, you try to put the collar/ harness and lead on your dog. She is now leaping up in the air, grabbing at your hands, twisting and turning. Plus, she is excitingly barking.

You get more and more frustrated, you are no longer calmly trying to tell her to calm down and some expletives burst from your mouth. That darned dog is just not staying still for one second.

Then the inevitable happens and your dog in all her excitement catches your hands with her teeth and nips you. You are now angry at her for getting so excited that she can't control her nipping. As a result of all these excited antics, the walk you are about to embark on will already be starting on a negative note.

Of course, the above scene is the worst possible scenario and I use it to illustrate my point. A dog that is already over-excited before the walk even starts is likely to be over-the-top for the entire walk.

The result is a dog that does as she pleases, one that does not listen to you. She pulls on the lead and the moment you release her in the field or park for a good run she is gone without a second glance at you.

If your dog is at all apprehensive of other dogs or people, she will be more likely to react in a negative way when you come across anyone on your walk. It is not the way anyone should or would want to start a walk with their dog.

By controlling excitement levels when you get ready for a walk, you can and will have an enormous impact on the quality of your walk and on how enjoyable it is going to be for you as well as your dog.

By investing in calmness in the home, not just at walk or feeding times, but throughout the day, you can start to control the level of excitement your dog has at any given time. Doing this will also teach your dog an important base level of self-control.

The Choice Game

If your dog gets overexcited when you go and put your shoes on, there is a very simple game that you can play to teach her to control her excitement. It is a little game that I like to call the Choice Game.

You will need a bowl of her normal food and if you like you can use a clicker to mark the correct choice, but don't worry if you don't like using one. You can use a marker word like "Yes" instead.

Step 1:

Take 5 to 8 treats and place them in the palm of your hand, closing your hand around them.

Step 2:

Hold your closed hand out towards your dog and let her investigate your hand. Your dog will likely lick, nibble, poke and perhaps even paw at your hand to try and work out how to get access to the treats.

Step 3:

Let your dog investigate until she backs off to have a think about how to get the treats. Open your hand. Your dog will now

try and dive in to grab the treats. When she does this close your hand again. Your dog will not get a treat at this stage.

Step 4:

Repeat step 2 to 3 until your dog no longer tries to dive in to get the food in your hand when you open it.

Step 5

Now take a piece of food from your open hand with your other hand and give it to your dog. If your dog moves forward to try and grab the food in your open hand close it and return the piece you have just taken back to the now-closed hand.

Step 6:

Keep repeating until your dog learns to sit back and let you deliver the pieces of food to her one piece at a time.

Step 7:

Keep repeating Steps 1 to 6 until your dog understands that showing self-control earns her access to the food.

Check out the Bonus at the end of this book for the next steps in this fabulous little game.

Once your dog has learnt the principles of the Choice game you can use it to control your dog's excitement when you are getting ready for your walks.

Simply place the treats on a surface where your dog can see them but is not able to reach them and then do the following:

When you go and get your shoes simply walk up and bend over to pick them up. The moment your dog gets excited, stop and wait for her to calm down. When she does, give her a treat from the pile of treats you prepared earlier.

Keep practising this until your dog stops getting excited as soon as you approach your shoes. Then work on bending down to pick your shoes up.

Keep working at this step by step, until you can put your shoes on without your dog getting excited.

Mixing up the routine can also have a positive effect as your dog will never know whether you're about to go for a walk, or whether you are just going to put your shoes on for no reason.

You should do the same exercise for any part of your getting ready routine that gets your dog excited. Once you have taught your dog not to get excited by your routine, you should start adding in other actions such as picking up the dog lead.

If your dog starts to get excited again simply hang it back on the hook and wait until she calms down.

If she chooses to stay calm during any of this process, of course, reward her with a treat and clip the lead on to her collar or harness.

Step 3: Keeping The Attention

In life, some things that we do are so easy that we don't need to concentrate on doing them, whilst others are more demanding and require our full concentration.

Our attention can drift and we can find ourselves getting distracted. Sometimes keeping your attention on the task at hand can be very difficult. Especially when there are lots of things going on around you that draw your attention away.

It doesn't really matter what these distractions are; an interesting story on the radio, a notification popping up on your phone, or maybe your husband/ wife or kids asking you a question.

Once you are distracted, you take your eye off the thing that you should be doing.

You deal with the question you are being asked, stop to listen to the radio or check out that notification on your phone.

The task you were supposed to be doing gets forgotten for the moment and you will get back to it when you are ready.
But even then, when you refocus your attention on the job that you are supposed to be doing, it will take you a while to get back into it, and until you are back in the flow of it, you are easier to distract.

It becomes kind of a vicious circle.

It is the same for your dog. For her, walking on a loose lead is not something that comes naturally.

It is something that she must learn.

For your dog to learn to walk on a loose lead she needs to learn a very important life skill, which we have already discussed in chapter 4.

The life skill that your dog needs to learn is Focus, keeping her attention on us when walking on the lead.

In this case, we will be looking for close focus. This is exactly what our next game "All Eyes on Me" teaches your dog.

All Eyes on Me

There are 2 levels to this game.

The first level teaches your dog to look at you.

The second level teaches your dog to keep her attention on you.

Your dog must master level 1 before you can move on to level 2.

In this game we are going to be teaching your dog to look at you and pay attention to you.

For this we need the following:

- A good amount of your dog's dry food or small tasty treats.
- Container or treat pouch.
- Optional: Clicker.

Level 1

Step 1:

Place a piece of food on the floor, and let your dog eat it.

Step 2:

Mark your dog (by clicking your clicker or saying "Yes") as soon as she looks back up at you, reward with a tasty treat.

Step 3:

In this step we are switching from placing the piece of food on the floor to dropping it instead. Allow your dog to eat it. Click or say "Yes" to mark your dog the moment she looks back up at you. Reward her with a treat.

Step 4:

Repeat. Mark and reward your dog each and every time she looks back up at you.

Level 2

Step 1:

Place a piece of food in your left hand and hold your hand up next to your face.

Step 2:

Wait for your dog to look at you and not your hand, click and reward.

Step 3:

Repeat until your dog is looking at you and ignoring your hand.

Step 4:

Repeat step 1 but, this time, hold the piece of food in your right hand.

Step 5:

Repeat steps 2 to 4 until your dog is looking at you, ignoring your right hand.

Step 6:

Now repeat steps 1 through to 5 but gradually move the treat-holding hand further away from your face.

Step 7:

Increase the difficulty again by holding the treat between your fingers so that your dog can see it as you move your hand about.

Step 8:

Repeat until your dog is a pro at ignoring the food in your hand and keeping her attention on you.

Step 4: Moving Together

Moving together is what walking on a loose lead is all about. This step is about teaching your dog to move with you in harmony. It is about teaching her to give in to the pressure on her neck and step back away from it rather than fighting against it. The following games teach your dog the key life skills of closeness, self-control and flexibility.

Teaching your dog to move with you in balance will result in a dog that not only behaves calmly but will be able to ignore distractions too. Instead we want your dog to reorient to you and not react to the distractions in the environment. It doesn't matter what the distraction is, a bird swooping down, leaf dancing in the wind or another dog walker coming around the corner.

Moving together is a skill that needs building and we have some cool games that focus on this when walking on a nice loose lead.

The Check Back Game

This game teaches your dog a solid foundation skill and helps her learn a variety of life skills. Key amongst these are Focus and Bouncebackability, which are two of the skills we need to teach for lead walking. This game will also have a positive effect on those needing more off-lead control, including coming when called.

This very simple game teaches our dogs to focus on us and the beauty of it is that it is quick to play. You can use your dog's breakfast or dinner to achieve great focus and amazing check backs. Initially, you start playing this game in your home, but as your dog progresses you can take it out into the garden and eventually you can take it on walks with you.

You will need the following:

- Your dog's normal food in a handy container. Alternatively, you can use treats but remember to adjust your dog's normal food allowance to compensate for the extra treats to prevent her from becoming overweight.
- A long lead for when practising outside.
- Optional: A clicker.

Step 1:

Grab a handful of your dog's food.

Step 2:

Throw a piece of food a few metres away from you and allow your dog to go and eat it. Wait for your dog to look back at you, mark the turn of the head towards you with an excited "Yes" or a click, and then throw another piece of food out.

Step 3:

Repeat step 2 a few times.

Step 4:

Repeat step 2 again, but this time wait for the head turn and a step in your direction, before marking with your excited "Yes" or a click. Then throw out another piece of food.

Step 5:

Repeat step 4 several times.

Step 6:

This time wait for your dog to take 2 steps towards you.

Step 7:

Keep playing the game and gently build up the distance your dog must come towards you before being rewarded. The aim is to have your dog checking back and returning to you for the game to continue.

Once your dog has understood this game, you can progress to teaching her to return to your side as soon as the lead goes tight.

The No Pressure Game

For this game, you need to have your dog on a lead. You are going to teach your dog to give in to the pressure that a tight lead puts on your dog's neck through her collar. For this game you are not pulling back on the lead, nor tugging at it, all we are doing is maintaining slight but constant tension on the lead until your dog moves away from the pressure she feels through her collar on her neck, towards you.

You will need the following:

- A collar or harness
- Normal walking lead
- A portion of your dog's normal food or tasty treats.
- Optional: Food Bowl. I normally place the piece of food on the floor, but you can place the food in a food bowl instead.

Step 1:

Clip the lead onto your dog's collar or Harness.

Step 2:

Place a piece of food on the floor in front of your dog but far enough away that she cannot get it. Your dog will want to go and eat the food and will move towards it.

This will put tension on the lead.

Hold firm and don't allow your dog to drag you over to the food. Maintain slight tension on the lead, but do not pull back to prevent your dog from getting the food.

Step 3:

Wait for your dog to turn her head towards you and move away from the food on the floor, click and reward giving her a treat from your hand.

Step 4:

Place some more food on the floor (or in the bowl) by the piece you put down before.

Step 5:

Maintain the slight tension on the lead and wait for your dog to give in to the pressure on her neck and come to you. Click and reward.

Step 6:

Place some more food on the floor (in the bowl) by the food already there. This will help to keep your dog interested in the food we have already placed on the floor. Maintain slight tension on the lead and when your dog checks back and looks at you allow your dog to go forward to get the food on the floor/ bowl.

Every now and again you are going to need to let your dog go forwards to eat the food you placed on the floor. We need to maintain the desire to move forwards towards the food on the floor, to be able to teach your dog to give into the pressure on her neck.

Step 5. Staying Together

In the previous step we started to teach our dog to come with us when we started moving. This step is all about asking your dog to move with you on a loose lead and to stay with you as you walk together.

You are teaching her that being, and staying, close to you is very rewarding. Thus, achieving your goal of having a dog that does not pull on a lead more quickly.

We want to teach our dogs to choose to stay with us. Regardless, of whether we are standing talking to a neighbour or walking along a road.

This element of walking on a loose lead encompasses learning to ignore distractions that will be popping up along the way. It is about teaching your dog the self-control she needs to choose you over the environment.

The first game that we have a look at in this step is called Close to Me.

Close To Me

Here we add value by inviting your dog to come as close to you as she can and build value by rewarding this closeness. When teaching this game to puppies I invite my puppy to climb all over me and reward her. I do this as it builds value in being close to me.

The more value your dog has for being close to you, the more likely it is that she will offer that behaviour again. For older dogs, we will be asking them to come as close as they, and you, are comfortable with.

For this game we need the following:

- High value treats, such as pieces of cheese or sausage.
- Container or treat pouch.

Step 1:

Prepare 10 high-value treats. We want these treats to be such high value that your dog gets all bright-eyed, bushy-tailed and wriggly about the prospect of having them.

Alternatively, you can use your dog's favourite toy to teach this concept.

Step 2:

Play with your dog and through the play get them to come really close to you. When they do, reward with a tasty treat.

Step 3:

Step away from your dog, a single step will do. Does she follow you and stay close? If she does, then reward her again.

Step 4:

Repeat step 2

Step 5:

This time turn away from your dog, wait for her to follow. If she does, then reward her.

Step 6:

Try and shape your dog to stand next to you instead of in front of you, using steps 2 – 4 to accomplish this. If your dog is really struggling with this you can use your hand to guide her to your side.

Step 7:

Repeat step 5 and step 6 a few times.

Step 8:

Move a few paces away from your dog. Can she follow you and return to your side? Reward if she does. You may need to wait a little while for her to find your side. Reward when she gets it.

If your dog is struggling with this step return to step 5 and practice that step a bit more before moving on to step 7.

The Ball Launcher Game

This game will teach your dog to stay by your side as you move together. It helps with Focus and Closeness. It will also strengthen your relationship with your dog.

I first started using this technique about 10 years ago. I used it to help owners of small dogs reward them, eliminating the need to have to bend over each time.

For this game you will need the following:

- A selection of soft treats such as cheese or pate
- A Ball Launcher. Ball not required.

Step 1:

Squish a piece of cheese or put a smear of pate into the cup of the ball launcher.

Step 2:

Present it to your dog and let her lick the cheese or pate out of the cup.

Step 3:

Put some more cheese or pate into the cup.

Step 4:

Now hold the cup a few inches from your dog's nose. Let her come forward. As soon as she moves forward to get the food from the cup, click and let her lick it to get the reward.

Step 5:

Refill, and this time add a little movement. You only need to move the ball launcher a foot or so. Can your dog follow the cup? Yes? Mark and reward by letting her have a lick.

Step 6:

Refill and add a little more movement. Again, as your dog follows the ball launcher, mark and reward.

Step 7:

Refill and start walking, resting the ball launcher across your legs so that the cup is by your left knee. Hold it steady in this position as you move. Mark and reward as your dog now moves with you.

Step 8:

Repeat step 7.

Tip: Try moving in a straight line, circles, weaving etc.

And finally

This chapter, the last in my book, gave you a 5-step process that will help you turn any lead walking struggles around. I am not promising that change will happen immediately. Each dog is an individual and some dogs will make quicker progress than others.

Don't let this discourage you from your efforts. As with any training, practice makes perfect and the more you follow the advice given in this book and teach your dog the practical exercises provided for you, the better the results will be.

Before we finish, I want to touch on one more point. I often get asked how long a training session should be and the answer might surprise you. I always tell my students to do short training sessions lasting about 5 minutes each, whenever they have a spare moment or 2. However you should aim to do at least 3 sessions a day.

There are a few good reasons for this:

It is easier to keep your dog's attention for a few minutes than it is for a one-hour training session.

Breaking down the training in small focused sessions will allow your dog to learn faster.

You are more likely to have the time to grab a handful of food and do a little bit of training with your dog than you are to be able to set aside a whole hour to train on a daily basis.

Now go and check out the special gifts I have prepared for you…

A Special Gift For You

I really hope you have enjoyed reading this little book and that it has inspired you to tackle your dog's lead pulling issues.

There are different learning styles out there, some people learn by reading, some by watching and others learn better by listening. This is a well-known fact and something I am acutely aware of and appreciate as a professional dog trainer.

For some people, this little book will be all the help they need to start turning their overexcited, train-pulling pooch into a model walking companion. For others though, the written word is not enough. They need some more practical help to start turning their struggles around.

This is why I have come up with some very cool bonuses that will help you get the most out of the information contained within this little book.

Bonus One

Never again will you worry about how to start your training session or what exercise to concentrate on next. Here is everything you need to do, and practice laid out in an easy to follow step by step plan that covers 3 weeks' worth of training. It tells you what you need to be practising each day.

I promise you will not have to put aside hours at a time to get all the games and training into your daily routine.

I am giving you free access to my "No Pulling Allowed" Training Plan, this plan is tried and tested and has helped countless of my dog training clients to turn their "back-breaking" and their "pulling my arm out of its socket" dog into a model walking companion.

To get access to this very cool free Bonus sign up now at www.nopullingallowed.co.uk/bookbonuses

Bonus Two

Free Access to the "No Pulling Allowed" mini video course.

As an additional and very cool bonus for simply being awesome, I am also giving you free access to my "No Pulling Allowed" Mini Video Course.

In this mini-course, I will show you exactly how to teach your dog to walk calmly by your side. The course is divided into five modules that cover the 5 steps to your dog becoming a model walking companion as described in this book.

Module 1 Preparing To Walk The Dog

There are a huge number of different collars, head collars and leads to choose from out there. You, as a dog owner, need to make the right decision about which piece of equipment to use. In this module we will be discussing the different pieces of equipment, what they are meant to do and compare them. We will have a look at the pros and cons of the different options and how, once you have made your choice, to introduce them to your dog.

Module 2 Before The Walk

Dogs get excited about the prospect of going for a walk. We need to control the excitement before starting the walk. In this module, we are going to have a look at what happens to a dog when they get overexcited at the prospect of going for a walk and how we can teach them to chill and be relaxed before we leave the house.

Module 3 Keeping Your Dog's Attention

The key to having a dog that doesn't pull on the lead is being able to keep their attention on you. In this module, I will teach you exactly how to teach your dog the all-important skill of Focus and reveal how you can become the most important thing in your dog's life.

Module 4 Moving Together

Once we have Focus, we need to teach our dogs that all the good things come from staying with us, even when we start moving together. In this module, I will be showing you exactly how you can teach your dog to stay next to you as we start to add a little movement.

Module 5 Staying Together

This is the module that combines all the skills that we have learned in the previous 4 modules and teaches you how to keep your dog's attention on you on a walk. I will show you how to do this in real life situation.

About the Author

As I sat down to write about who I am so you can get to know me a little better, I started to wonder what you would actually like to know about me.

I had a look at how other authors talk about who they are and why they do what they do. In fact, I spent most of this afternoon looking at the many books I have in my collection, I was hoping to draw inspiration from those who came before me.

However, having looked at most of them, it struck me that most authors "About Me" sections are, quite frankly, boring. And I don't want you to be bored when you read about me.

No, instead I want to inspire you, to show you that you too can solve your dog's problems just like I did. At times we all need a little help. Sometimes, knowing that you are not alone will inspire you more than a boring bio would. Do you really need to know that I was born in Holland, that I currently live in Dorset, am married to a wonderful guy named Paul and that, at the time of writing this book, I have 3 BSD Groenendaels?

Instead, I decided to share with you the story about how I became a dog trainer.

You see 24 years ago, I was just like you, an ordinary puppy owner who had collected a wriggly, fluffy and very energetic puppy from, in my case and to my shame, I must admit, a puppy dealer. In those days I didn't know diddly squat about puppies or dogs for that matter.

But when we brought our little Sheltie pup home, this was soon to change.

I thought I was doing the right thing, taking 2 weeks off to settle our new pup in. For days we struggled to find a name for our little boy, but in the end, after watching the "Teenage Mutant Ninja Turtles" on TV, we decided to go for an artist's name and as I really admire the Surrealist Salvador Dali we settled on calling him, Dali. I spent every minute of those 2 weeks with him.

Oh, how I enjoyed his cute puppy antics for those two weeks.

Unfortunately, as soon as I had to return to work things started to go wrong.

At the time I worked full time, just around the corner from where we lived. I felt very lucky to be able to go home at lunchtime to go and walk Dali and spend some time with him.

We struggled a little with the toilet training in the first couple of weeks, as the 4 hours I had to leave him for in the morning were just a tad too long. But as he grew that problem resolved itself.

Unfortunately, he did discover that the door frames were a fabulous chew toy and that the walls when licked became soggy and then he could dig holes in them. I'm making light of this now, but at the time it was a sign that Dali was not coping when we left him alone.

He had been spoilt by me being there for him every single day for the first two weeks.

I had no clue that what you were supposed to be doing was teaching a puppy that it is OK to be on their own.

His separation anxiety was one of the reasons I started looking for answers. The other reason was that, although I was reading a lot of books on dog training, trying to teach him using the pictures from the books as my instruction, not knowing what I was doing meant that Dali wasn't reacting to me the way the dogs in the books did.

I managed to teach him to sit and lie down but teaching him to walk on a loose lead or come when I called him appeared to be beyond me.

These problems prompted me to find a local dog training club to see if they could help.

I was lucky to find such a club in the next village. I went along and joined their puppy class and learnt how to train Dali. I spoke to the instructors there and got help with Dali's separation anxiety and became more and more interested in training dogs and dog behaviour. It wasn't long before I joined the clubs committee and became one of their volunteer trainers.

A long-life passion was born and as time has passed, I have gathered more and more knowledge and understanding about what makes dogs tick.

And now I have the joy of sharing that experience, passion and knowledge with other dog owners like you.

Other Books by the Author

Dogz Thinkz Differentz: Considering Dog Behaviour and Training Terminology (in collaboration with Anna Patfield, Helen Hitchin and Mandy Daveridge)

Books in the Fun | Focus | Play Dog Training Series (1 – 2)

No Pulling Allowed - From Painfully Disappointing Drag to Delightfully Relaxing Stroll.

Reliable Racing Recalls (due for release late 2019)

Where to find me

If you would like more direct help from me or would like to book me for a workshop or seminar you can contact me via email at natasja@nightsabredogtraining.co.uk.

Details of my weekly classes and how to book a private lesson can be found at: www.nightsabredogtraining.co.uk

My Fun | Focus | Play Blog can be found at: www.nightsabredogtraining.co.uk/blog

You can find my Online Video Courses at www.funfocusplay.co.uk

I also have a YouTube channel, which you can find at https://www.youtube.com/channel/UCogVeJmuTqux2hH7Z45tJGg